Unit 2 Adverbs

Adverbs tell us more about verbs.
*He approached the dog **cautiously**.*
*She walked **quickly** across the room.*

1. Complete these sentences with a suitable **adverb** from the wordbank.

   clearly   joyfully   dimly   silently   hurriedly   greedily

   a) He ate _____.
   b) She shouted _____.
   c) He ran _____.
   d) The teacher explained _____.
   e) The light shone _____.
   f) He crept _____.

2. Make **adverbs** from these adjectives by adding **-ly**.

   a) quick _____
   b) slight _____
   c) soft _____
   d) rapid _____
   e) bright _____
   f) painful _____
   g) sudden _____
   h) immediate _____

3. Choose five of the **adverbs** you have made. Use each one in a sentence.
   _____
   _____
   _____
   _____
   _____

4. Complete these sentences with a suitable **adverb**.

   a) He laughed _____.
   b) She drew the picture _____.
   c) The moon shines _____.
   d) They waited _____.
   e) He slept _____.
   f) The river flows _____.

Unit 3 The past tense (1)

Most verbs form their **past tense** by adding **-ed**.
wash — wash**ed**   paint — paint**ed**

1. Change these verbs into the **past tense**.

a) cook _____   b) whisper _____

c) cover _____   d) count _____

Verbs ending in **e**, drop the **e** before adding **-ed**.
hop**e** — hop**ed**   smok**e** — smok**ed**

2. Change these verbs into the **past tense**.

a) wipe _____   b) move _____

c) phone _____   d) slice _____

Some short verbs **double** the **last letter** when adding **-ed**.
rub — rub**bed**   stop — stop**ped**

3. Change these verbs into the **past tense**.

a) trip _____   b) trot _____

c) pin _____   d) sob _____

Other verbs form their **past tense** in **different ways**.
bring — brought   shake — shook

4. Change these verbs into the **past tense**.

a) make _____   b) go _____

c) write _____   d) stand _____

5. Change these verbs to the **past tense**. Use each one in a sentence of your own.

a) cross _____

b) rescue _____

c) drop _____

d) buy _____

e) sell _____

f) wear _____

g) swim _____

Unit 4   Double consonants

a b c d e f g h i j k l m n o p q r s t u v w x y z

The letters **a, e, i, o, u** are called **vowels**. **All other letters** are called **consonants**.

What do you notice about the **consonants** in bold type in this sentence?
*He built a co**tt**age in the mi**dd**le of a field.*

The consonants in bold are **double consonants**.

1. Underline the **double consonants** in the words below.

bubble	follow	kettle	traffic
slipper	bigger	dinner	ladder
missing	puzzle	summer	butter

2. Use each word in a sentence of your own.

   _____
   _____
   _____
   _____
   _____
   _____
   _____
   _____
   _____
   _____

Unit 5   More confusing words

Here and hear

Here means **this place**.
Come over **here**.

Hear is something you do when you **listen**.
I can **hear** music.

The word h<u>ear</u> has <u>ear</u> inside it!

1. Complete with **here** or **hear**.

   a) Did you _____ the good news?

   b) We _____ you're interested in fishing.

   c) I _____ he will be coming _____.

   d) Do you _____ what I _____.

   e) _____ we are.

New and knew

New is the **opposite** of **old**.
She bought some **new** shoes.

Knew is the **past tense** of **know**.
I **knew** all the answers.

2. Complete with **new** or **knew**.

   a) She _____ when he would be coming.

   b) He _____ you had bought a _____ car.

   c) Is that dress _____?   d) I _____ it was!

3. Use each word in a sentence of your own.

   a) here _____

   b) hear _____

   c) new _____

   d) knew _____

4. Complete these sentences with the correct word.

   a) I can _____ the _____. (sea/see)

   b) Tell me a _____ of a puppy dog's _____. (tale/tail)

   c) She bought a _____ at the market _____. (plaice/place)

   d) What did the ear hear? Only the _____ _____. (knows/nose)

Unit 6 Animal homes and families

1. Match the **animal** to its **home**.
   Rewrite the list of **homes** in **alphabetical order**.

Animal	Home	Alphabetical order
horse	kennel	_____
pig	burrow	_____
bird	shell	_____
bee	sty	_____
wild rabbit	nest	_____
tame rabbit	stable	_____
lion	hive	_____
snail	den	_____
dog	hutch	_____

2. Complete the list of animal families below with words from the wordbank.

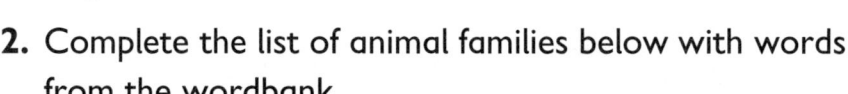

> kid   lioness   gander   nanny-goat   bitch   ram
> rooster   chicken   calf   cub   mare   gosling
> bull   foal   puppy   piglet   lamb   sow   drake

Animal	Male	Female	Young
duck	_____	duck	duckling
sheep	_____	ewe	_____
dog	dog	_____	_____
cattle	_____	cow	_____
goose	_____	goose	_____
fowl	_____	hen	_____
goat	billy-goat	_____	_____
horse	stallion	_____	_____
lion	lion	_____	_____
pig	boar	_____	_____

7

Unit 7 — Correcting mistakes

1. Rewrite these sentences correctly.

   a) We've all catched a cold.

   b) Was you late?

   c) Bren and Stuart is going to school.

   d) Listen what I am saying.

   e) She brung some cakes from the shop.

   f) Were are you going? Too town?

   g) He spoke loud.

   h) He hurted his leg.

   i) I did the job when I am ready.

   j) There is three pencils missing.

   k) They swimmed all afternoon.

2. Underline the spelling errors in these sentences. Rewrite the sentences correctly.

   a) I carn't ear properely. I think I'm gowing def.

   b) How wood you liek having a damp cushon too sit on?

   c) I've got a teribul cold in the hed allredy.

   d) He doesn't cur abowt us. He nocks evryone over.

   e) As sumwon brokin intwo youre home?

   a) _____
   b) _____
   c) _____
   d) _____
   e) _____

8

Unit 8   The Daily News

Write a news report to go with each headline.

THE DAILY NEWS

PM sees Loch Ness monster

World record shattered

Weather warning

Unit 9

Changing tense

Change this commentary in the present tense to a past tense report.

The procession is coming along Queen's Road. The crowd's waving. Police on motorcycles are at the front. A marching band follows them. They are playing a stirring tune which brings a smile to everybody's face. Fathers hold up young children. They get a good view that way.

The first float approaches. It is decorated with flowers and carries children from a local school. They are dressed as Romans. They smile at the people who line the route. After them a second float brings the magic of the Caribbean. The sound of a steel band makes everyone happy. They listen and tap their feet. They clap in time to the music. The sun comes out. Everyone begins to cheer. It is a beautiful sight.

Unit 10   The past tense (2)

Most verbs make the **past tense** by adding **-ed**.
*play — play**ed**   shout — shout**ed***

Other verbs make their **past tense** in **different ways**:

Present tense	Past tense
break	broke
speak	spoke
buy	bought
bring	brought
know	knew
go	went
take	took
make	made
drink	drank
begin	began

Write a short sentence using the **past tense** of these verbs.

1. go _____
2. take _____
3. speak _____
4. buy _____
5. bring _____
6. know _____
7. begin _____
8. drink _____
9. break _____
10. make _____

Unit 11 Spelling

always started better almost number stopped never also still

1. Sort the above words into these patterns.

   al   **st**   **er**

   _____   _____   _____
   _____   _____   _____
   _____   _____   _____

2. Use each of the above words in the wordbank in a sentence of your own.

   _____
   _____
   _____
   _____
   _____
   _____
   _____
   _____
   _____

3. Use the **look**, **say**, **cover**, **write**, **check** method to learn the spellings of the above words.

12

Unit 12 Synonyms

A **synonym** is a word which has the same or nearly the **same meaning** as another word.

A **thesaurus** is a book which **lists synonyms**.

1. Find synonyms for these words.

frightened	see

strong	laugh

2. Choose two words from each list and use each one in a sentence of your own to show its meaning.

Unit 13   Exploring word order

Look at this sentence from "**The Bogeyman**" by Jack Prelutsky.

In the desolate depths of a perilous place the bogeyman lurks, with a snarl on his face.

The word order in this sentence can be changed in different ways and yet still keep the same meaning.

With a snarl on his face, the bogeyman lurks in the desolate depths of a perilous place.

The bogeyman lurks, with a snarl on his face, in the desolate depths of a perilous place.

The bogeyman lurks in the desolate depths of a perilous place, with a snarl on his face.

Rewrite these sentences in three different ways, keeping the meaning the same.

1. Without hesitation, he dived into the clear waters of the lagoon..

   _____
   _____
   _____

2. Silently, he crept into the room.

   _____
   _____
   _____

3. Carrying the box carefully, he walked down the lane.

   _____
   _____
   _____
   _____

Unit 14 Past and present tense

Rewrite this extract, changing it from the **past tense** to the **present tense**.

I was leaning back on my hands, starting to feel better. My right hand started to itch.

I reached to scratch it and brushed something away.

And I realized my legs were itching, too. And felt something crawling on my left wrist.

I shook my hand hard. "What's going on here?" I whispered to myself.

My entire body tingled. I felt soft pinpricks up my arms and legs.

Shaking both arms, I jumped to my feet. And banged my helmet against a low ledge.

The light flickered on.

I gasped when I saw the crawling creatures in the narrow beam of light.

Spiders. Hundreds of bulby, white spiders, thick on the chamber floor.

They scuttled across the floor, climbing over each other. As I jerked my head up and the light swept up with it, I saw that the stone walls were covered with them, too.

from *Return of the Mummy,* by **R. L. Stine**

Unit 15 — A space alien

In *The Spaceball*, Maggie Freeman describes what her alien looks like, how he feels to the touch and how his voice sounds.

Describe and draw an alien creature of your own. Make your description as clear and real as you can.

Unit 16 — Plurals

Words ending in f

When a word ends in **f**, the **f** is changed to **ve** before adding **s**.

shelf — shelves   wolf — wolves

1. Make these words **plural**.

   a) loaf _____   b) leaf _____

   c) life _____   d) calf _____

   e) half _____   f) knife _____

   g) wife _____   h) scarf _____

2. Choose four of the **plurals** you have made and use each one in a sentence.

   _____
   _____
   _____
   _____

Male and female

boys — girls   lions — lionesses
men — women   lords — ladies

Add **s** or **es** to make these words plural, then complete the list of male and female pairs below.

| goddess | sister | bride | queen | abbess |
| actress | aunt | duchess | waitress | princess |

Male	Female	Male	Female
kings	_____	bridegrooms	_____
actors	_____	waiters	_____
dukes	_____	uncles	_____
princes	_____	gods	_____
brothers	_____	abbots	_____

17

Unit 17

Definitions

The **definition** of a word is its **meaning**.

Write your own definitions of these words <u>in no more than three words.</u>

Word	Definition
ice	
feed	
year	
mud	
pebble	
soft	

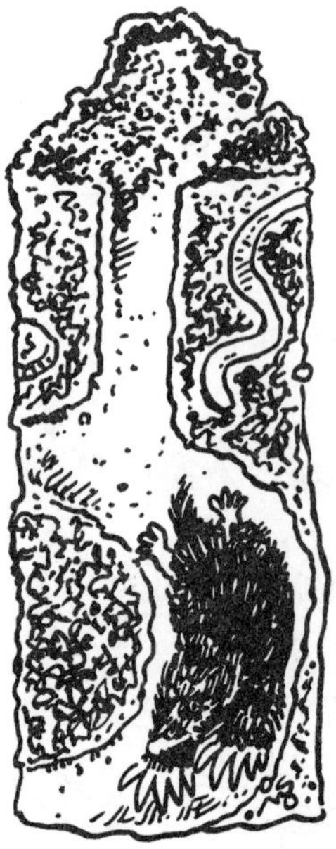

Word	Definition
underground	
entrance	
safe	
fine (pieces)	
fine (weather)	
to plug	

Word	Definition
rapidly	
tiny	
grip	
grow	
prevent	
protect	

Unit 18 Spelling

1. Complete these sentences. The missing words all end in **-ack**.

   | sack black slack crack back pack |

   a) She had a _____ and white cat.

   b) He put the potatoes into a _____.

   c) I must _____ my suitcase for the holiday.

   d) He arrived _____ home at six o'clock.

   e) Another word for loose is _____.

   f) The egg began to _____ open.

2. Complete these sentences. The missing words all end in **-ock**.

   a) You wear a _____ on your foot.

   b) The ship has just come into _____.

   c) The _____ struck ten.

   d) A _____ is a very large stone.

   e) Don't play with electricity, or you will get a _____.

3. Find the word ending in **-tch**.

   a) To go to get something and bring it back is to _____.

   b) If you have an itch you will need to _____.

   c) An organised game of football is a _____.

   d) A cage for a pet rabbit is a _____.

   e) To take hold of a ball when it is moving is to _____.

   f) A _____ is made with a needle and thread.

   g) A piece of material used to cover a hole in clothing is a _____.

   h) A channel at the side of a road to drain water is a _____.

   i) An item worn on your wrist to tell the time is a _____.

   (Check all your spellings in a dictionary!)

19

Unit 19 — The apostrophe: belonging to

A raised comma like this ' is called an **apostrophe**. It is often used to show that something belongs to someone.

Joanne's trainers   *Dad's car*

Note that the **apostrophe** comes after Joanne but before the **s**.

1. Rewrite these using an apostrophe. The first one has been done for you.

   a) The birthday of Darren   <u>Darren's birthday</u>

   b) The book belonging to Nikki _____

   c) The car owned by my aunty   _____

   d) The tail of the dog   _____

   e) The brush used by the artist _____

If the owner word already ends in **-s** or **-es** then we add an apostrophe only.

The ladies' dresses   *The teachers' cars*

2. Rewrite these using an apostrophe. The first one has been done for you.

   a) The shoes of the boys   <u>The boys' shoes</u>

   b) The cries of the babies   _____

   c) The song of the birds   _____

   d) The honey of the bees   _____

   e) The spades of the gardeners _____

3. Fill in the missing apostrophes.

   a) Staceys brother is friendly with Bills cousin.

   b) The teachers chairs were set out by Ahmeds uncle.

   c) The babies prams were bought from Toms shop.

   d) Mr Smiths car is newer than my uncles.

   e) Helens dad borrowed his neighbours lawn mower.

Unit 20 Proofreading

Proofreading is **checking written work** for mistakes and **making corrections**.

1. Underline the spelling mistakes in this passage. Rewrite the passage with the correct spellings.

   It was allmost harf past too in the mourning. Suddinly I herd the door opin. My bruther came in. "Their's somthing outsied," he sed, "lisen." I jumpt owt of bed. There was a lowd sownd and then a secand won. We opinned the winder and lookt out. Sumthing was moving in the gardin.

2. Rewrite this passage with **correct punctuation**.

   when school was over and she had done her homework joanna asked mrs jennings if she could take her dog rolf for a walk her neighbour was delighted

   of course you can she said itll save me half an hour ive so much work to do getting the house ready for when my brothers family comes from australia

   when do they arrive joanne asked

   ten oclock saturday morning

21

Unit 21 — Missing letters

k or **v**?

1. Complete these words with **k** or **v**.

   a) ___an   b) ___ey
   c) ___itten   d) ___olcano
   e) ___eep   f) ___oice
   g) ___isit   h) ___itchen
   i) ___alley   j) ___ind
   k) ___illage

2. Choose two words beginning with **k** and two beginning with **v**. Use each in a sentence of your own.

   _____
   _____
   _____
   _____

Wo or **wa**?

3. Complete these words with **wo** or **wa**.

   a) _____ter   b) _____rd
   c) _____rm   d) _____rld
   e) _____rn   f) _____lk
   g) _____sh   h) _____nder

4. Choose two words beginning with **wo** and two beginning with **wa**. Use each in a sentence of your own.

   _____
   _____
   _____
   _____

Unit 22 — Words with ss

1. Make these male words female with an **-ess** ending.

   a) prince <u>princess</u>   b) lion _____

   c) host _____   d) steward _____

   e) waiter _____   f) actor _____

   g) tiger _____   h) god _____

2. Choose three of the words you have made and use each in a sentence of your own.

   _____
   _____
   _____

3. All these words have **ss** in them. What are they?

   a) a name for a cat: p_____
   b) the opposite of hit: m_____
   c) very fast: ex_____
   d) the sound a snake makes: h_____
   e) an item of clothing: dr_____
   f) sickness: i_____
   g) we drink out of these: g_____
   h) delivered by a messenger: m_____
   i) a corridor: pa_____
   j) it is written on an envelope: a_____
   k) to have: po_____
   l) a secret word: pa_____

4. Choose five of the words in question 3, and use each in a sentence of your own.

   _____
   _____
   _____
   _____

Unit 23 Suffixes (1)

A **suffix** is a letter or **letters** added to the **end** of a word to make a new word.

1. Make as many words as you can by adding some of these endings.
   The first one has been done for you.

   | -ful | -fully | -ive | -tion | -ly | -less | -or | -er | -est | -ness |

   a) play   playful playfully player
   b) care   _____
   c) act   _____
   d) firm   _____
   e) near   _____
   f) direct _____
   g) pain   _____
   h) rough   _____

2. Choose one of the new words you have made from each word above. Use each in a sentence of your own.

   _____
   _____
   _____
   _____
   _____
   _____

Unit 24 — Spelling and sound

Some words have the **same spelling pattern** but **different pronunciations**.

we**ar**: h**ear** **ear** cl**ear**

st**one**: **one** d**one**

s**ai**d: p**ai**d m**ai**d pl**ai**d pl**ai**t

1. Collect words to complete this chart.

	Same spelling, same sound	Same spelling, different sound
gr**ow**	low mow show tow know	how now cow town
st**one**		
g**ive**		
y**ea**r		
al**ive**		

Some words have the **same sound** but **different spellings**.

s**o**cks: b**o**x f**o**x

sk**y**: l**ie** h**igh** b**ye** b**uy**

m**ee**t: s**ea**t tr**ea**t wh**ea**t

2. Collect words to complete this chart.

	Same sound, same spelling	Same sound, different spelling
b**ear**	tear pear wear	share where there stair chair
tr**y**		
c**ou**ld		
f**ou**r		
t**ough**		
r**ight**		
s**uch**		

25

Unit 25 — Word endings

1. Collect words with these common endings.

-tion	**-sion**	**-ive**
attention	vision	attentive

-ible	**-our**	**-ough**
invisible	hour	rough

-able	**-ould**
comfortable	could

2. Use some of the words you have collected in sentences of your own.

Unit 26 Overworked words

Some words are overworked. Underline the overworked word in this passage.

Dad went to the pet shop and bought a puppy and brought it home and gave me a lovely surprise. It wagged its tail and licked my face and pushed its nose into mine and I gave it a bowl of water and Mum put some meat in another bowl and we watched it have its dinner.

1. Re-write the passage so that you use **and** as few times as possible.

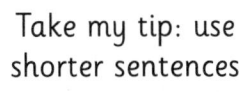
Take my tip: use shorter sentences

_____
_____
_____
_____
_____

2. Another overworked word is **then**. Re-write this passage so that you use **then** as few times as possible.

Tom rushed home from school. Then he had his tea. Then he did his homework. Then he phoned his friend and then they decided to go swimming. Then he asked his mum's permission. Then she said he could and then he ran upstairs for his swimming things and then he went to the pool with his friend. Then they swam for half an hour. Then they came home. Then Tom watched TV and then he went to bed.

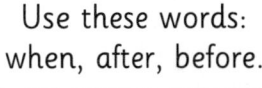
Use these words: when, after, before.

_____
_____
_____
_____
_____

Unit 27 Suffixes (2)

1. Make new words from these words by adding a **suffix**. Use each suffix only once.

Words	Suffixes	New words
act	-ful	_____
cruel	-ly	_____
pain	-y	_____
rust	-able	_____
ant	-ive	_____
enjoy	-ment	_____
violin	-ic	_____
attach	-ist	_____

2. Choose six new words. Use each in a sentence of your own to show its meaning.

_____
_____
_____
_____
_____
_____

3. Add a suffix to complete these words.

tear_____   pian_____   making a state_____

28

Unit 28 Compound words

A **compound word** is a word made from **two other words**.

1. Find the two words which make these **compound** words. The first one has been done for you.

   a) cupboard   cup board   b) handbag   _____

   c) pinprick   _____   d) headlamp   _____

   e) everywhere _____   f) bookcase   _____

   g) overboard   _____   h) waterfall _____

2. Build eight **compound** words by joining words from the word bank.

   | room week down thing end toe self head |
   | any bed stairs line noon tip after my |

   a) _____   b) _____
   c) _____   d) _____
   e) _____   f) _____
   g) _____   h) _____

3. Do the same as question 2 with these words.

   | birth some up sun foot news |
   | light pass night thing to stairs |
   | step day port paper |

   a) _____   b) _____
   c) _____   d) _____
   e) _____   f) _____
   g) _____   h) _____

4. Choose three compound words and use each one in a sentence.

   _____
   _____
   _____

Unit 29   All change!

1. Change these **statements** into **questions**.

   a) I start every day the Crunchy Wheat way.

   _____

   b) No breakfast cereal is healthier.

   _____

   c) All the goodness is left in.

   _____

   d) This incredible robot actually thinks for himself.

   _____

   e) You won't be disappointed.

   _____

   f) You pay only £3.99.

   _____

2. Change these sentences to give them an **opposite meaning**.

   a) You'll agree that Crunchy Wheat is delicious.

   _____

   b) When Robo sets off, put the remote away. You won't need it.

   _____

   c) Nothing is taken away. All the goodness is left in.

   _____

   d) Robo is the toy everybody wants. Stocks are limited.

   _____

   e) Collect the special coupons. You pay only £3.99.

   _____